ANCIENT JEWISH PRAYERS AND THE MESSIAH

Dr. Richard Booker

ANCIENT JEWISH PRAYERS AND THE MESSIAH

Printed in the United States of America

ISBN: 0-9711313-5-X
978-0-9711313-5-4

Acknowledgment:

A special prayer of gratitude to our Father in heaven for giving Peggy to me. She has been a faithful wife and prayer partner since 1966. She is not only the greatest wife in the world; she is also the best Christian I know. Whatever I may have accomplished and whatever blessing I may have been to others, it is because of her.

I want to also acknowledge Dr. Marvin Wilson for reading the manuscript and making valuable suggestions. Marv, *todah*!

Table of Contents

1
THE JEWISH BACKGROUND TO CHRISTIAN PRAYERS

Since the New Testament is a continuation of the First Testament, we should understand that the Hebrew Bible is the foundation to Christian prayers. By the time of Jesus, there were 2,000 years of Hebrew/Jewish history, culture, language, traditions, customs, and prayers that formed the background to the New Testament. As a *Torah*-observant Jew, Jesus lived His life, practiced His faith, and prayed within the context of the Jewish culture of His day.

In the New Testament period, there were prescribed prayers written centuries earlier that Jews prayed at the Temple, the Synagogue and in the privacy of their homes. Jesus would have prayed these prayers as well as His own personal prayers.

When Jesus taught His disciples to pray, He did not give them Western cultural instructions. Instead, He taught them the heart of Jewish prayers and gave godly wisdom on attitudes and practices in prayer. Biblical New Testament Christianity inherited these prayers, much of which are still prayed today by Jews in their synagogues from their prayer book.

In order to pray biblically, Christians can learn much from ancient Jewish prayers, their place in the New Testament, the way Jews pray today, and the connection of Jewish prayers to Christian prayers. In this chapter we will learn Jewish views of prayer, the *Shema*, Jewish blessings and the *Kaddish,* a powerful prayer exalting God often prayed in times of great sorrow and tribulation such as the death of a loved one.

In Chapter 2, we will study the *Amidah*, which is the central prayer in Jewish life. In Chapter 3, we will study the most famous Jewish prayer in Christendom, the "Lord's Prayer."

Jewish Views of Prayer

1. Jewish Prayer is Personal and from the Heart

While Christian prayers are sometimes written in advance for special occasions, believers more often pray impromptu prayers at the moment prayer is requested or expected. Many Christians don't have a tradition of saying prayers that are prepared beforehand or memorized for every occasion. They pray "on the spur of the moment."

Because Jewish prayers are written in a prayer book called a *Siddur*, Christians sometimes believe that Jewish prayers are routine prayers of ritual that come from the lips rather than from the heart. While this can certainly be true in Christianity as well as Judaism, (for example, Christians who repeat the "Lord's Prayer" without an understanding of what they are praying), Jewish prayer is called, "service of the heart."

In his publication, "The Lonely Man of Faith", the late Rabbi and scholar Joseph B. Soloveitchik wrote, "... the very essence of prayer is the covenantal experience of being together with and talking to God and that the concrete performance such as the recitation of text represents the techniques of implementation of prayer and not prayer itself

("The Lonely Man of Faith," *Tradition* 7:2, Summer 1965, page 35).

Jesus prayed the prescribed prayers of His time such as the *Shema,* the *Amidah*, and the blessings. He also prayed impromptu prayers. Whatever the forms of prayer Jesus prayed, He certainly prayed them out of His heart and not out of ritual.

A written prayer that is based on the Bible can be just as spiritual and heartfelt as a spontaneous prayer. Christians can embrace prescribed prayers written by godly leaders because they give depth and guidance to our praying. I encourage you to study the prayers in the Bible and then write your own prayers based on the insights you receive as you study the biblical prayers.

2. Jewish Prayer is Corporate

Whereas Christian prayer emphasizes the individual (give me), Jewish prayer is community oriented (give us). We learn this in the "Lord's Prayer" where Jesus taught His disciples to pray: *Our* Father … give *us* … forgive *us* … deliver *us* … . We see this community mindset in the Jewish prayer expression, *Avinu, Malkeinu*, which means, "*Our* Father, *Our* King."

The idea of community is found in the traditional Jewish concept of requiring a *minyan* of at least ten men in order to have a public service. This comes for the book of Genesis where Abraham interceded for Sodom and asked God to spare the city if there were just ten righteous within the city (Genesis 18:32). While most of the prayers in the

Siddur can be prayed alone at home, even then, they are expressed within the framework of community.

Christian individualism is a Greco-Roman concept not found in the Bible. When Christianity severed its Hebraic root, it lost the understanding and practice of community. While we Christians cherish and take pride in our individualism, deep down inside, most of us yearn to be part of a community of loving, caring people.

Unfortunately, our Western cultural presentation has so emphasized the personal side of salvation; we have lost the concept and ability to relate as a covenant people. When we are born again by God's Spirit, we become part of a family. We are not saved to ourselves but to the Lord and His people.

Our prayers, attitudes and actions should not only be personal but should also express the understanding that we are part of a community. We are members of the household of faith. We are joined to others in the body of the Lord and the Kingdom of God. What concerns others should concern us. We have a responsibility to one another. Furthermore; we have been grafted into the Jewish people and have become part of the Commonwealth of Israel.

3. Jewish Prayer is Focused

Jewish prayer is also focused. In his wonderful book, *To Pray as a Jew*, Rabbi Hayim Halevy Donin writes, "Reading from a prayer book does not mean that one is praying. One may read a prayer book as one reads any other kind of book—to find out what it says or to relish the beauty of the poetry. Such reading does not qualify as prayer. To transform reading into prayer, there must be at least a sense of standing in the presence of God and the intent to fulfill one of His commandments" (page 19).

The Hebrew word for focus, direction and intent is *kavanah* (spiritual zeal). It means to set your heart towards God with a passion to know Him, to hear His voice, to discover His will and do His will. It calls the worshipper to put aside all worldly distraction so as to better concentrate on the Almighty and the prayer offered to Him. *Kavanah* requires the worshipper to prepare himself/herself before praying.

The Jewish worshipper is exhorted to "know before Whom you are standing." Those who would approach the Almighty in prayer must come before Him in a reverent frame of mind. There is no place for irreverence, and foolish, frivolous attitudes and prayers. Before praying, the worshipper should meditate on the greatness of God and remove all thoughts of worldly matters and pleasures. The goal is to shift one's focus away from self and towards God.

A servant would not approach a king with a sad countenance. Likewise, if a person is downcast or in a bad mood, he or she should sing a psalm, hymn or spiritual song in order to approach God in a spirit of joy. As we learn in Psalm 100:2, "Serve the LORD with gladness; come before His presence with singing".

Judaism teaches that prayer without *Kavanah* is like a body without a soul. It is empty ritual. *Kavanah* requires the mind to be disciplined and focused in order to properly reverence God, to discover His vision for your life and to pray specific prayers that will help you fulfill your goals and objectives.

The Apostle Paul was thinking of *Kavanah* when he wrote, "If then you were raised with Christ (Messiah), seek those things which are above, where Christ (Messiah) is sitting at the right hand of God. Set your mind on things above, not on things of the earth" (Colossians 1-2).

Taken in its Hebraic context of prayer, Paul also said, "speaking to one another in psalms and hymns and spiritual songs, singing and making melody in your heart to the Lord" (Ephesians 6:19).

As we apply the powerful Hebraic concept of *Kavanah*, the veil of separation will be split allowing us to enter the presence of the Holy One and reach His heart in prayer.

4. Jewish Prayer Emphasizes the Kingdom of God

While Christian prayers are often preoccupied with material needs and possessions, Jewish prayers emphasize spiritual concerns. They focus on seeing the fullness of the Kingdom of God manifested on the earth. The sages of old who wrote the prayers did not concern themselves with the things of this world. They had a burning passion for the sovereign rule and kingship of God in heaven to be fully realized on the earth.

Whereas Christian prayers often express concern for individual salvation, Jewish prayers petition the Almighty to destroy wickedness and establish righteous and justice on the earth. They are much more kingdom minded than Christian prayers, which are generally limited to a local and personal view.

While Jewish prayers certainly petition the Almighty for help with personal needs, their primary emphasis is to see God's redemptive purposes fulfilled on the earth as they are in heaven. They express the desire for God to rule and reign in Israel, and from there, to the nations. Their focus is kingship, lordship, sovereignty and rule over the nations, more so than personal issues.

"Rabbi Chaim of Volozhin explains that the true purpose of prayer is to increase God's influence over the world. We ask for blessings from His hand so that His kindness will permeate the world with greater intensity. The supplicant uses genuine prayer as a springboard, propelling himself heavenward to new spiritual heights, even while remaining physically on the earth" (Rabbi Avrohom Chaim *Feuer, Shemoneh Esrei*, page 46).

This is the way Jesus taught us to pray. He said to pray, "Our Father in heaven, Hallowed by Your name. Your kingdom come. Your will be done on earth as it is in heaven" (Matthew 6:9-10). This is not a Christian prayer. It is a Jewish prayer that we have inherited as followers of a Jewish Lord.

Jesus also said, "But seek first the kingdom of God and His righteousness, and all these things shall be added to you" (Matthew 6:33).

Paul's prayers in the New Testament are powerful spiritual prayers. They do not emphasize physical needs and material comforts because the Lord knows we have these needs and has promised to provide for them. Christian prayers should reflect a good balance between kingdom concerns and personal issues.

5. Jewish Prayers are Mostly in Hebrew

While some Jewish prayers are in Aramaic, they are mostly in Hebrew. Hebrew is the holy tongue of the prophets, the language of the Bible, the "sacred tongue" (*lashon hakodesh*). Prayers in Hebrew written in the *Siddur* forge the link between the covenant people of God in biblical times and Jews of modern times. For this reason, prayers prayed collective at the synagogue are mostly in Hebrew.

Rabbi Donin explains that the great benefit of praying prayers from the *Siddur* in Hebrew is, "A Jew may choose his own words when praying to God; but when he uses the words of the Siddur, he becomes part of a people. He identifies with Jews everywhere who use the same words and express the same thoughts. He affirms the principle of mutual responsibility and concern. He takes his place at the dawn of history as he binds himself to Abraham, Isaac, and Jacob. He asserts his rights to a Jewish future in this world, and to personal redemption in the world-to-come" (Rabbi Hayim Halevy Donin, *To Pray as a Jew,* Page7).

Rabbi Donin also notes that while Hebrew is the preferred language in Jewish prayers, Jews may individually pray their own prayers in any language. God honors the heart. Rabbi Donin recalls the following story to illustrate this point.

"A boy from a small rural village where there were few

Jews and no synagogue, one day accompanied his father to the city to do some marketing. While they were there, they went into a synagogue. The boy had never been in a synagogue before and was impressed and moved by the sight of the congregation at prayer. He too, wanted to pray. But he did not know how. His father had taught him only to say the letters of the Hebrew alphabet, but no more than that. So a thought occurred to him. He began to recite the alphabet over and over again. And then he said, 'O Lord, You know what it is that I want to say. You put the letters together so they make the right words' "(page 17).

In the rest of this chapter, we will learn to pray some basic prayers in Hebrew. In doing so, we can find our own identity as people of the covenant who are grafted into the Jewish people and the Commonwealth of Israel. Even though you may be just learning how to pronounce the Hebrew, the Lord will put the letters together to make the right words. May it please our Rabbi in heaven to hear His new covenant children praise Him in the *lashon hakodesh*, the holy tongue of the prophets.

The Shema

The Jewish declaration of faith is called the *Shema* (meaning 'hear') based on Deuteronomy 6:4. It reads, "Hear, O Israel: The LORD our God, the LORD is one!" In Hebrew it is pronounced, *Shema, Yisrael, Adonai Eloheynu, Adonai Echad.* This confession, along with Deuteronomy 11:13-21 and Numbers 15:37-41, was repeated as a daily prayer morning and evening by observant Jews in their personal prayers, at the Temple and was incorporated into synagogue worship.

When the priests read the *Shema* as part of the Temple service, the people would respond by saying, *Baruch shem kvod malkhuto l'olam va-ed,* which means, "Blessed is the name of His glorious kingdom forever and ever."

Because He was raised by godly Jewish parents and perfectly kept all the commandments, Jesus would have prayed the *Shema.* Since Jesus prayed this prayer, it is important to learn what it means and to pray it in Hebrew. By doing so, we can connect with Jesus and the Jewish people to declare our faith in the God of Abraham, Isaac, and Jacob.

Shema Yisrael

This declaration begins with the exhortation: *Hear, O Israel.* This opening statement tells us that the God of the Jews is a personal God for He asks us to listen to Him, which would not be possible if God was simply a force or power without personality. It also tells us that God wants to communicate with us and that we can hear Him.

Adonai Eloheynu

The second part of the declaration is: *The LORD our God.* This statement is important because it identifies God by His name. The word "God" is generic and can refer to any deity. The ancient world had many gods. The only way to know which god they worshipped was to identify the particular god by name.

When the God of the Bible identified Himself to Moses He revealed His name by saying, *I AM WHO I AM* (Exodus 3:13-15). This most unusual name in Hebrew is spelled *YHWH or YHVH* and means "the One who is actively present." God's name in Hebrew is the *yud, hay, vav, hay.* The four letters are called the Tetragrammaton, which means a word of four letters.

God's name was so sacred to the Hebrews they were afraid to even pronounce it. When the Hebrews wanted to use God's name, they substituted the word *Adonai (LORD)* or *Hashem*, which means, "the Name"). However, the word Lord also refers to God's rule over His creation. When they wrote about God, the Hebrews had to have some way to distinguish when they were talking about His name and when they were talking about His rule.

When the Bible was translated into English, the word YHWH was put in all capital letters (LORD) when it referred to God's name and lower case Lord when it referred to His rule.

Hebrew Bible scholars called the Massoretes added vowel points to the Hebrew Scriptures to help us pronounce the words. During the Reformation period, Gentile Bible scholars misunderstood these vowel points and thought God's name was pronounced as Jehovah. Ever since then, Christians have used this name when addressing the God of the Bible.

The Hebrew word used in the *Shema* for God is *Eloheynu*. This is a plural form of the word which is translated into English as "our God." We will learn later the significance of God being "our God."

Adonai Echad

These words tell us that the *LORD is One*. There is more to this statement than meets the eye because of the meaning of the word "One." There are two Hebrew words used in the Scripture that are translated into English by the word one. One word is *yachid.* This word means absolute unity as in "only one." For example, we see the use of this word in Genesis 22:2 where God says to Abraham, "... Take now your son, your only son Isaac ..." . Isaac was the one and only child of Abraham by Sarah.

Another Hebrew word for one is *echad.* This word means one in the sense of a composite unity. We find this word used, for example in Genesis 2:24 which reads, "Therefore shall a man leave his father and mother and be joined to his wife, and they shall become one flesh." Adam and Eve were two different personalities but they were one in that they came together in unity as one flesh.

This information suggests to us that, while there is only one God, He exists as a collective unit which Christianity understands as a Trinity but would be better understood by the word "*echad*." The fact that God is a composite unity is suggested in the most fundamental statement of faith in Judaism. He is the One God of Abraham, Isaac, and Jacob who exists in more than one personality.

Reciting the Shema

Jewish sages teach that there are both 248 parts in the human body and 248 positive commandments in the *Torah.* This symbolism suggests that we should use our entire body to obey God's holy *Torah*. The total number of words in the three Scriptures repeated for the *Shema* is 245. In order to complete the symbolism, the sages added three words to it which are said prior to reciting the *Shema*.

The three words in Hebrew are *El melekh n'eman*, which means God, Faithful King. God is the All-Powerful King who rules as sovereign Lord and He is faithful to keep His covenant promises. Christians are very familiar with the translation of these three words: the *aleph*, the *mem*, and the *nun*. They spell out the Hebrew word "Amen."

El melekh n'eman

Shema Yisrael, Adonai Eloheynu, Adonai Echad

Baruch shem kvod malkhuto l'olam va-ed

Blessings (*Berachot*)

When God created the universe, He was so pleased with the results that He said it was very good (Genesis 1:31). He blessed (*baruch*) Adam and Eve and gave them dominion over the earth (Genesis 1:28). From that original blessing, God set the example of blessing (*berachah*) as the means for mankind to magnify Him and extend His blessings to others. As a result, people routinely blessed God in their worship and prayers and one another in their social interaction with people.

When God called Abraham, He blessed him and said that Abraham would be a blessing to others (Genesis 12:1-3). God would bless (*barach*) Abraham, his descendants and the world through them with the revelation of the One True God, the written Scriptures, and the Messiah. Because they were chosen to bless and be blessed, the practice of blessing God became central to all Jewish prayers. Blessing people became the common means of extending His favor to others.

When God's people blessed others, they were not speaking meaningless words just to be polite. They believed they were declaring the purposes of God and the goodness of God to the one they were blessing. They fully believed that by their faith and obedience, God would impart that which was spoken to the person. His presence and power would be released to fulfill the blessing. Since they were God's covenant people made in His image, they had the authority and right to receive and extend His blessings to others.

Because the New Testament is a Jewish book, we see the concept of blessing God and others in its pages. Jesus blessed God (Matthew 15:36) and people (Matthew 5:3-12). The apostles blessed God and blessed people (Ephesians 1:3). We too are called to bless God and extend His blessings to others.

Blessing God

Our priority in prayer is to bless God. But how can creatures bless the Creator? What do we have that God needs? The answer is absolutely nothing. While the word bless generally means praise, its more precise meaning is to increase, expand, and intensify like a river overflowing its banks.

When we bless God, we are declaring that He is the source of all blessing and that we desire the overflow of His glory, His power, and His provision to increase, expand, and intensify in our lives, in the lives of others, and throughout the world. This will find its ultimate fulfillment at the end of the age when the glory of God will cover the earth as the waters cover the sea. His glory will not be contained but will overflow to cover the world.

Until this final increase of the glory of God, we are to follow the example of King David who said, "I will bless the LORD at all times; His praise shall be continually in my mouth" (Psalm 34:1). David also wrote, "Bless the LORD, O my soul; and all that is within me, bless His holy name! Bless the LORD, O my soul, and forget not all His benefits: who forgives all your iniquities, who heals all your diseases. Bless the LORD you His angels, who excel in strength, who do His word. Bless the LORD, all you His hosts, you ministers of His, who do His pleasure" (Psalm 103:1-3, 20-21).

Another word that means basically the same is magnify. Psalm 34: 3 reads, "Oh, magnify the LORD with me, and let us exalt His name together".

The Jewish people took this literally and composed one hundred blessings that could be said everyday. These blessings express honor to God and recognize His sovereignty and goodness in all areas of life that most of us take for granted.

There are blessings for awakening in the morning, blessings for washing the hands, blessings for food and drink, blessings for bodily functions, blessings for the family, blessings for the events of life, blessings for the beauty of creation, blessings for the Sabbath and the festivals, blessings when doing a mitzvah, etc. Through these blessings, the Jewish people learned that they did not bless things, but God who is the source of all things good and bad.

In the New Testament, we find Jesus blessing God for the food (Matthew 26:26-27), Paul blessing God and His people (Ephesians 1:3), and Mary and Cornelius and his household magnifying God (Luke 1:46; Acts 10:46).

Paul expressed this idea of blessing God when he wrote "pray without ceasing, in everything give thanks …" (1 Thessalonians 5:17-18). He also wrote, "giving thanks always for all things …" (Ephesians 5:20). What a wonderful way to be reminded that God is the source of all blessings.

Blessing Prayers

The beginning words of the blessing are always the same and are followed by a statement that relates to the occasion for the blessing. The wording in Hebrew is as follows:

Baruch Ata Adonai, Eloheynu Melech Ha-olam.

Baruch – blessed, praised, magnified, increase, expand, intensify

Atah – are you

Adonai Eloheynu – O LORD Our God (personal, intimate)

Melech Ha-olam – King of the universe (sense of awe)

Blessing Over Bread "Hamotzi"

Ba-ruch A-ta A-do-nai E-lo-hey-nu Me-lech Ha-o-lam,

Blessed are You, O LORD our God, King of the Universe,

Ha-mo-tzi Le-chem Meen Ha-a-retz.

Who brings forth bread from the earth.

Blessing Over the Wine

Ba-ruch A-ta A-do-nai E-lo-hey-nu Me-lech Ha-o-lam,
Blessed are You, O LORD our God, King of the Universe,
Bo-reh Pri Ha-ga-fen.
Who Creates the Fruit of the Vine.

Blessing Over Fruit Which Grows on Trees

Ba-ruch A-ta A-do-nai E-lo-hey-nu Me-lech Ha-o-lam,
Blessed are You, O LORD our God, King of the Universe,
Bo-reh Pri Ha-etz.
Who Creates the Fruit of the Trees

Lighting the Shabbat Candles

Ba-ruch A-ta A-do-nai E-lo-hey-nu Me-lech Ha-o-lam,
Blessed are you O LORD our God, King of the Universe,
A-sher Kid-sha-nu Be-mitz-vo-tav,
Who has sanctified us with His commandments,
Ve-tzi-va-nu Le-had-lik Ner Shel Shabbat
and commanded (inspired) us to kindle the light of Shabbat.

Blessing Others

Not only are we to bless God, we are also to bless others. God Himself gave us a command to bless others and even gave us the words. We know this as the priestly blessing but it is really God's blessing He gave to us as His priests to give to others.

We read in Numbers 6:22-27 "And the LORD spoke to Moses, saying: Speak to Aaron and his sons, saying, This is the way you shall bless the children of Israel. Say to them 'The LORD bless you and keep you; the LORD make His face shine upon you, and be gracious to you; the LORD lift up His countenance upon you, and give you peace.' So shall they put My name on the children of Israel, and I will bless them."

Jesus said, "Bless those who curse you, and pray for those who spitefully use you" (Luke 6:28). Paul wrote, "Let no corrupt word proceed out of your mouth, but what is good for necessary edification, that it may impart grace to the hearers" (Ephesians 4:29-30).

James said, "But no man can tame the tongue, It is an unruly evil, full of deadly poison. With it we bless our God and Father, and with it we curse men, who have been made in the similitude of God. Out of the same mouth proceed blessing and cursing. My brethren, these things ought not to be so" (James 3:8-10).

When we bless others, we extend the favor of God to them and declare that His will be done in their lives. As we observe and discern the call and gifting of God in others lives, we acknowledge that call and gifting and speak a release of God's grace and provision.

Peter blessed God and he blessed people. He said, "Blessed be the God and Father of our Lord Jesus Christ (Messiah) …"(1 Peter 1:3). He further said, "Finally all of you be of one mind, having compassion for one another; love as brothers, be tenderhearted, be courteous; not returning evil for evil or reviling for reviling, but on the contrary blessing, knowing this that you were called to this, that you may inherit a blessing" (1 Peter 3:8-9).

A sample blessing might be as follows:

The LORD bless you and keep you. The LORD make His face shine upon you, and be gracious to you. The LORD lift up His countenance upon you, and give you peace. May the Spirit of the Lord, the spirit of wisdom, the spirit of understanding, the spirit of counsel, the spirit of power, the spirit of knowledge, and the spirit of the fear of the Lord rest upon you.

You would then pray the specific blessing appropriate for the individual as the Lord reveals it to you.

Kaddish

The *Kaddish* is an ancient Jewish prayer in Aramaic glorifying God. It is often prayed in times of mourning at the death of a loved one. Jewish people recite this prayer as an expression of their faith in the Almighty to take their burdens and comfort them as they mourn the loss of their loved ones.

May His great Name grow exalted and sanctified in the world that He created as He willed. May He give reign to His kingship in your lifetimes and in your days, and in the lifetimes of the entire family of Israel, swiftly and soon. Amen.

Blessed, praised, glorified, exalted, extolled, mighty, upraised, and lauded be the Name of the Holy One. Blessed is He beyond any blessing and song, praise and consolation that are uttered in the world. Amen.

May there be abundant peace from Heaven, and life, upon us, and upon all Israel. Amen.

He who makes peace in His heights, may He make peace upon us, and upon all Israel. Amen.

Kaddish

Yit-ga-dal ve-yit-ka-dash she-mei ra-ba be-al-ma di-ve-ra chi-re-u-tei,

Ve-yam-lich mal-chu-tei be-cha-yei-chon u-ve-yo-mei -chon u-ve-cha-yei de-chol beit

Yis-ra-eil, ba-a-ga-la u-vi-ze-man ka-riv, ve-i-me-ru: a-mein.

Ye-hei she-mei ra-ba me-va-rach le-a-lam u-le-al-mei al-ma-ya.

Yit-ba-rach ve-yish-ta-bach, ve-yit-pa-ar ve-yit-ro-mam ve-yit-na-sei, ve-yit-ha-dar

ve-yit-a-leh ve-yit-ha-lal she-mei de-ku-de-sha, be-rich hu, le-ei-la min kol

bire-cha-ta ve-shi-ra-ta, tush-be-cha-ta ve-ne-che-ma-ta, da-a-mi-ran be-al-ma, ve-i-me-ru: amein.

Ye-hei she-la-ma ra-ba min she-ma-ya ve-cha-yim a-lel-nu ve-al kol Yis-ra-eil, ve-i-ru: a-mein.

O-seh sha-lom bim-ro-mav, hu ya-a-seh sha-lom a-lei-nu ve-al kol Yis-ra-eil, ve-i-me-ru: a-mein.

Early versions of the *Kaddish* included the phrase, "and cause His salvation to sprout and bring near His Messiah." It reads as follows: "... in the world He created according to His will; and may He establish His kingship (and cause His salvation to sprout and bring near His Messiah) during your lifetime and during your days and during the lifetime of the entire family of Israel, swiftly and soon..."

2
THE AMIDAH

In Chapter 1, we learned Jewish principles of prayer, the *Shema*, and the concept and importance of blessing God and others. We also learned some basic prayers in Hebrew plus the *Kaddish*. In this chapter, we will study the most important prayer in Judaism, the *Shemoneh Esrei* or more popularly referred to as the *Amidah*.

The primary sources I consulted for the information on the *Shemoneh Esrei* are: 1) "To Pray as a Jew: A guide to the Prayer Book and the Synagogue Service" by Rabbi Hayim Halevy Donin, (Basic Books, 1980) 2) "The ArtScroll Siddur," Mesorah Publications, (1984, 1987, 1990) and 3) "Shemoneh Esrei" by Rabbi Avrohom Chaim Feuer, (Mesorah Publications, 1990, 1995).

The Siddur

Along with the Hebrew Bible and the *Talmud*, the *Siddur* is the most important book in Judaism. Simply put, the *Siddur* is the Jewish prayer book. But it is much more than that. The word *Siddur* means "order." It is the printed order of prayers collected over time and organized in such a way to guide Jewish people in their praying on the Sabbath and weekdays. Eventually, these prayers were compiled and published in written form.

According to Rabbi Wayne Dosick, "The first systematic *Siddur* was outlined by Rab Amram ben Sheshna Gaon in the Academy of Sura in Babylonia in 870 C.E.

"Less than a century later, the great Rabbi Saadya Gaon (882-942 C.E.) compiled a more complete, more logical *Siddur*, which to this day still serves as the basic format for Jewish prayer" (Rabbi Wayne Dosick, "Living Judaism," HarperCollins Publishers, NY, 1995, page 116.)

The core prayers in the *Siddur* were composed by ancient Jewish sages and represent their combined efforts to write prayers that were based on the biblical revelation of the nature, character and purposes of the God of Abraham, Isaac, and Jacob. Some of these prayers were written before the time of Jesus. As *Torah*-observant Jews, Jesus, His disciples, and the Apostle Paul would have certainly prayed these prayers. Later prayers that withstood the test of time, and became universally accepted by the Jewish leadership and people, were added to the prayer book.

Overtime, the wisdom and content of the prayers in the *Siddur* became a primary means for teaching Jewish doctrine, history and faith and values to the "people of the book." They are universal prayers of thanksgiving, praise and worship, confession, and petition that express the yearnings of the Jewish people in seeking the Creator for their spiritual, emotional, physical, material, and corporate concerns.

Shemoneh Esrei (Amidah)

The most important prayer in the *Siddur* is called the *Shemoneh Esrei*, which means "eighteen." The prayer was given this name because the original version consisted of eighteen blessings. Judaism teaches that the prayer was composed by the 120 men of the Great Assembly in the fifth century BC.

The blessings and structure of the prayer was formalized after the Temple was destroyed. This was around 90 AD. At this time a nineteenth blessing was either added or revived for the purpose of cursing groups that did not conform to what the sages considered normative Judaism. In the second century, this would include, but not be limited to the Jewish followers of Jesus, who by then, were considered heretics. This request was made by Rabbi Gamliel II, who was the grandson of Gamliel of the New Testament. He was Paul's teacher and the leader of the Sanhedrin who saved the lives of the disciples (Acts 5:33-39).

The prayer is most commonly known as the *Amidah*. *Amidah* means "standing." The prayer is called by this name because it is said while standing. Because this is the most popular name for the prayer, it is the name used in this chapter.

The *Amidah* is a powerful prayer to the Almighty. When the members of the Great Assembly sought to compile a prayer for the Jewish people, they compiled words and phrases from the Hebrew Bible that would express their faith, hopes and needs. The *Amidah* became the universally accepted prayer in Judaism. It is the standard liturgy prayed by Jews around the world, much like the "Lord's Prayer" is in Christianity.

As a *Torah*-observant Jew, Jesus would have prayed the original *Amidah*. In fact, as we will learn in the next chapter, the "Lord's Prayer" appears to be a summary of the core elements found in the *Amidah*. While unique to the

Jewish people, and with some clarification, the *Amidah* certainly expresses the yearnings of believing Christians who are also the spiritual children of Abraham through faith in Jesus. May the God of Abraham, Isaac, and Jacob open our spiritual eyes to behold His glory as we study this powerful, timeless prayer.

Structure of the Amidah

The prayer consists of three sections. The first section is praise to God and includes three blessings. The middle section is petition to God and includes thirteen blessings. The first six of these blessings relate to personal needs. The next six relate to national Israel. The thirteenth blessing asks God to accept the prayer. The third section is thanksgiving to God. It too includes three blessings followed by a petition that God would accept the prayer.

Taken as a whole, the blessing elements incorporate the same kinds of prayers found in Christianity as well as the personal and corporate needs of all who worship the God of Abraham, Isaac, and Jacob. We would expect this to be the case since true biblical prayers are universal to both Jews and Christians. The primary difference, of course, is the Christian recognition of Jesus as the Messiah, Redeemer, Mediator, and Intercessor.

The following outline of the *Amidah* shows the structure of the prayer with the order and name of each blessing. Observant Jews pray this prayer three times a day. A shortened version containing seven blessings is prayed on Shabbat and at festivals.

The Blessings of Shemoneh Esrei (Amidah)

Preliminary Preparatory Prayer
(Approaching God in Prayer)

FIRST SECTION
The First Three Blessings – Praising God

Blessing 1 - The Fathers – Patriarchs
Blessing 2 - God's Power and Might
Blessing 3 – God's Holiness

MIDDLE SECTION
Petitions – Personal and Nationalistic and Summary Prayer

A. PERSONAL PETITION

Blessing 4 - Knowledge-Wisdom-Understanding
Blessing 5 - Repentance
Blessing 6 - Forgiveness
Blessing 7 - Redemption and Deliverance
Blessing 8 - Health and Healing
Blessing 9 - Material Prosperity

B. NATIONAL PETITIONS

Blessing 10 - Ingathering of Exiles

Blessing 11 - Restoration of Justice Righteousness

Blessing 12 - Destruction of God's Enemies

Blessing 13 - Prayer for the Righteous

Blessing 14 - Rebuilding-Restoration of Jerusalem

Blessing 15 - Coming of Messiah-Davidic Reign

C. SUMMARY PRAYER

Blessing 16 - Prayer of Acceptance

THIRD SECTION

The Last Three Blessings – Thanking God

Blessing 17 – Restoration of Temple Worship

Blessing 18 – Thanksgiving

Blessing 19 – Peace

Concluding Prayer

(May Our Prayer be Acceptable to God)

Preliminary Preparatory Prayer

"O Lord, open my lips, and my mouth shall show forth Your praise. For You do not desire sacrifice, or else I would give it; You do not delight in burnt offering. The sacrifices of God are a broken spirit, a broken and a contrite heart—These, O God, You will not refuse" (Psalm 51:15-17).

Before we pray, it is important to ask God for divine assistance. Our mind and heart must be focused on God as we seek to praise Him, petition Him, and thank Him. This need for divine enablement in prayer is recognized by both Christians and Jews and may be expressed with the prayer of David quoted from the Psalm.

Rabbi Feuer writes the following explanation, "God the Omnipresent, is everywhere; and yet, so to speak, He took a fragment of His spirit and embedded it within a human body. This is the human soul. The sliver of God constantly yearns to reattach itself to its Divine source, but the human body is a physical obstruction which interferes.

"However, at the times ordained for prayer the supplicant "strips his body away from his soul" so that the soul may embrace its source. Thus prayer is not man speaking to God—it is the God inside man speaking to the God outside of man. Therefore, the introduction to prayer is a plea for God to open our lips and remove all physical impediments to the dialogue between the Divine within us and the Divine all around us.

"When man, so frail and insignificant stands before his Maker and contemplates His praises, he should be struck silent with awe. Therefore, man must appeal for Divine assistance to open his mouth and endow it with the ability to declare God's praises" (pages 41-42).

Since the Apostle Paul was a *Torah*-observant Jew familiar with this prayer, he wrote of the same need for divine assistance when we pray, as we learn from the following Scriptures.

"For what man knows the things of a man except the spirit of the man which is in him? Even so no one knows the things of God except the Spirit of God. Now we have received, not the spirit of the world, but the Spirit who is from God, that we might know the things that have been freely given to us by God. The things which we also speak, not in words which man's wisdom teaches but which the Holy Spirit teaches, comparing spiritual things with spiritual.

"But the natural man does not receive the things of the Spirit of God, for they are foolishness to him; nor can he know them, because they are spiritually discerned" (1 Corinthians 2:11-14).

"Likewise the Spirit also helps in our weaknesses. For we do not know what we should pray for as we ought, but the Spirit Himself makes intercession for us with groanings which cannot be uttered" (Romans 8:26).

Blessing 1 – The Fathers – Patriarchs

The first blessing begins by acknowledging that God is the source of all blessings, and the worshipper desires that His person, presence and plans be magnified. Jewish people approach God on the basis of the covenant with their forefathers.

Moses made the same appeal to God when he interceded for the people when they were worshipping the golden calf. Moses prayed, "Remember Abraham, Isaac, and Israel …"(Exodus 32:13).

While Jewish people appeal to God on the basis of the merits of the patriarchs, they must still find their own personal relationship with God. We see this in the song of Moses when God split the Red Sea. They praised God with these words, "The LORD is my strength and my song, and He has become my salvation; He is my God and I will praise Him; my father's God, and I will exalt Him" (Exodus 15:2).

God is acknowledged as the Supreme Most High Creator who is awesome in His majesty, extends loving kindness to His people, redeems them and protects them for His name's sake.

Blessed are You, HASHEM, our God and the God of our forefathers, God of Abraham, God of Isaac, and God of Jacob; the great, mighty, and awesome God, the supreme God, Who bestows beneficial kindness and creates ever-thing, Who recalls the kindness of the Patriarchs and brings a Redeemer to their children's children, for His Name's sake, with love. O King, Helper, Savior, and Shield. Blessed are You, HASHEM, Shield of Abraham.

Blessing 2 – God's Power and Might

This wonderful blessing acknowledges the power and mercy of God to sustain life, heal the sick, deliver the oppressed, comfort those who mourn, provide needed rain to replenish the earth, and resurrect the dead. The hope in the resurrection is repeated five times.

While not a major theme in the Hebrew Bible, Job said, "For I know that my Redeemer lives, and He shall stand at last on the earth; and after my skin in destroyed, this I know, that in my flesh I shall see God" (Job 19:25-26).

Michael, the guardian angel of Israel, comforted Daniel with these words, "And many of those who sleep in the dust of the earth shall awake, some to everlasting life, some to shame and everlasting contempt. But you, go your way till the end; for you shall rest, and will rise to your inheritance at the end of the days" (Daniel 12:2,13).

The encouraging blessing of affirmation is:

You are eternally mighty, my Lord, the Resuscitator of the dead are You, abundantly able to save. (He makes the wind blow and He makes the rain descend,) He sustains the living with kindness, resuscitates the dead with abundant mercy, supports the fallen, heals the sick, releases the confined, and maintains His faith to those asleep in the dust. Who is like You, O Master of might deeds, and who is comparable to You, O King Who causes death and restores life and makes salvation sprout! And You are faithful to resuscitate the dead. Blessed are You, HASHEM, Who resuscitates the dead.

Blessing 3 – God's Holiness

God is separate from His creation. He is holy. In the song of Moses the people sang, "Who is like You, O LORD, among the gods? Who is like You, gloriousness in holiness, fearful in praises, doing wonders?" (Exodus 15:11). Hannah sang, "There is none holy like the LORD …" 1 Samuel 2:2).

God's works and way are holy (Psalm 145:17; Isaiah 55:8-9). His character is holy (Habakkuk 1:13). His people are holy (Exodus 19:5-6; Leviticus 19:2). God's holy name is sanctified in His people as they praise Him and live holy lives (Isaiah 57:15). The blessing reads as follows:

You are holy and Your Name is holy, and holy ones praise You everyday, forever. Blessed are You, HASHEM, the holy God.

Blessing 4 – Knowledge-Understanding-Wisdom

Once we have worshipped God, we petition Him for our needs. These six petitions relate to the personal needs of the worshipper. They are in the proper order in that the first three address spiritual needs while the last three relate to practical needs. Wisdom leads to repentance. Repentance leads to forgiveness. Forgiveness leads to redemption and deliverance. Redemption and deliverance lead to health and healing. Health and healing lead to material prosperity.

God created humankind with a soul that gives us the ability to think and reason. This is one of God's own qualities (created in His image) that sets us apart from the rest of His creation. Therefore, asking God to give us the grace to have knowledge (information), understanding (the meaning of the information) and wisdom (the application of the information) is the first blessing in this section of spiritual petitions.

The worshipper is seeking the mind of God (the divine perspective). This comes from the Word of God, as we learn from Solomon who was granted this gift, "If you seek her as silver, and search for her as for hidden treasures; then you will understand the fear of the LORD, and find the knowledge of God. For the LORD gives wisdom; from His mouth comes understanding; He stores up sound wisdom for the upright …" (Proverbs 2:5-7). "The fear of the Lord is the beginning of wisdom, and the knowledge of the Holy One is understanding" (Proverbs 9:10).

The fourth blessing reads:

You graciously endow man with intellect and teach insight to a frail mortal. Endow us graciously from Yourself with intellect, insight, and wisdom. Blessed are You, HASHEM, gracious Giver of intellect.

Blessing 5 – Repentance

Godly knowledge leads to an understanding of the moral character of God and the wisdom to see our personal need for repentance. God influences or helps us repent through His Word, by His Spirit, and the trials of life. We acknowledge that God is both our sovereign Lord and Father Who is full of mercy towards those who turn to Him.

King David expressed this for us: "Have mercy on me, O God, according to Your loving-kindness; according to the multitude of Your tender mercies, blot out my transgressions. Wash me thoroughly from my iniquity, and cleanse me from my sin" (Psalm 51:1-2). "As a father pities his children, so the LORD pities those who fear Him" (Psalm 103:13).

Repentance is more than lamenting. It is a turning away from our sins of omission and commission and seeking the grace and mercy of God to receive us. The fifth blessing asking God to help us repent reads as follows:

Bring us back, our Father, to Your Torah, and bring us near, our King, to Your service, and influence us to return in perfect repentance before You. Blessed are You, HASHEM, Who desires repentance.

Blessing 6 – Forgiveness

When we turn to God in repentance, He is ready to forgive us. He is a loving Father Who shows mercy to those who seek Him with their whole heart. Isaiah writes, "Seek the LORD while He may be found, call upon Him while He is near. Let the wicked forsake his way, and the unrighteous man his thoughts; let him return to the LORD, and He will have mercy on him; and to our God, for He will abundantly pardon" (Isaiah 55:6-7).

In this sixth blessing, the worshipper again acknowledges God both as King and Father. As King, God rules as sovereign Lord and Master to Whom we should show reverence. As Father, He is gracious and ready to forgive.

Forgive, us, our Father, for we have erred, pardon us, our King for we have willfully sinned; for You pardon and forgive. Blessed are You, HASHEM, the gracious One Who forgives abundantly.

Blessing 7 – Redemption and Deliverance

Now that the worshipper has petitioned God for spiritual needs, it is appropriate to ask God for assistance at the practical level. The following three blessings relate to deliverance from personal suffering of the soul and spirit, health and healing for the body and material prosperity.

God is concerned about our total well-being, spirit, soul, and body. Redemption is an on-going work of God in our lives on a daily basis and not just a climatic event when Messiah comes at the end of the age. We need to be redeemed everyday.

King David writes, "The righteous cry out, and the LORD hears, and delivers them out of all their troubles. The LORD is near to those who have a broken heart, and save such as have a contrite spirit. Many are the afflictions of the righteous, but the LORD delivers them out of them all" (Palm 34:17-19).

God will comfort us in our sufferings, deliver us in our times of distress, and defend us against our enemies. This is the essence of the seventh blessing which reads:

Behold our affliction, take up our grievance, and redeem us speedily for Your Name's sake, for You are a powerful Redeemer. Blessed are You, HASHEM, Redeemer of Israel.

Blessing 8 – Health and Healing

God is a healer of the spirit, soul, and body. Solomon explains, "Do not be wise in your own eyes; fear the LORD and depart from evil. It will be health to your flesh, and strength to your bones" (Proverbs 3:7-8). Jeremiah adds, "Heal me, O LORD, and I shall be healed; save me, and I shall be saved, for You are my praise" (Jeremiah 17:14).

The blessing for healing is based on God's power and compassion to make His people whole. He desires to heal us of the sins of the spirit, the sorrows of the soul, and the sicknesses of the body. It reads:

Heal us, HASHEM,—then we will be healed; save us—then we will be saved, for You are our praise. Bring complete recovery for all our ailments, for You are God, King, the faithful and compassionate Healer. Blessed are You, HASHEM, Who heals the sick of His people.

Blessing 9 – Material Prosperity

God is not only concerned about our spiritual and physical well-being; He also cares about our financial health. While the Bible constantly warns us against greed, God is a good God who desires to bless His children in all areas of our lives

God gives us wisdom to use our resources to bless Him and others. Proverbs reads, "Honor the LORD with your possessions, and with the firstfruits of all your increase; so your barns will be filled with plenty, and your vats will overflow with new wine" (Proverbs 3:9-10).

This blessing of petition for God's material provisions reads as follows:

Bless on our behalf—O HASHEM, our God—this year and all its kinds of crops for the best, and give (blessing/dew and rain for a blessing) on the face of the earth, and satisfy us from Your bounty, and bless our year like the best years. Blessed are You, HASHEM, Who blesses the years.

Blessing 10 – Ingathering of Exiles

The following six blessings are nationalistic and relate to the final ingathering of the Jewish people to the Land of Israel, the restoration of a just-righteous society, the destruction of Israel's enemies, the reward of the righteous, the rebuilding of Jerusalem and the coming of the Messiah who will establish the promised Kingdom of David. Israel will take her rightful place as the head of nations (Deuteronomy 28:1,13), Messiah will rule the nations from Jerusalem (Zechariah 9:9-10), and peace will finally come to the earth (Isaiah 2:1-4). (See Amos 9:13-15.)

Christians view Bible prophecy differently based on how they interpret the Bible. Those who have a literal view understand these prophecies to be for the Jewish people at the end of the age, and that they will culminate in the coming of the Messiah. Christian Zionist believe the modern ingathering is the fulfillment of these prophecies. The primary difference is the recognition of the Messiah.

Jewish tradition teaches that the ram Abraham sacrificed in place of Isaac had two horns. The smaller left horn was sounded at Mount Sinai while the larger right horn will be sounded by God to call the Jewish people in the *Diaspora* back to Israel. This is a way of saying that God will speak to the Jewish people in ways that will give them the desire to make *Aliyah*.

Isaiah writes, "So it shall be in that day; the great trumpet [shofar] will be blown; they will come, who about to perish in the land of Assyria, and they who are outcasts in the land of Egypt, and shall worship the LORD in the holy mount at Jerusalem" (Isaiah 27:13).

As the prophets declare, God will bring the exiles back to their ancient land as the banner to which the Jewish people will rally. Isaiah writes, "He will set up a banner for the nations, and will assemble the outcasts of Israel, and gather together the dispersed of Judah from the four corners of the earth" (Isaiah 11:12).

This blessing calling the Jewish people home reads:

Sound the great shofar for our freedom, raise the banner to gather our exiles and gather us together from the four corners of the earth. Blessed are You, HASHEM, Who gathers in the dispersed of His people Israel.

Blessing 11 – Restoration of Justice-Righteousness

For centuries the Jewish people have suffered under the injustices of anti-Semitism. When they return to their own land, their cry to the Almighty is His blessing of righteous leaders who will rule with His justice for the people.

Jeremiah speaks of these times as says, "Behold the days are coming, says the LORD, that I will raise to David a Branch of righteousness; a King shall reign and prosper, and execute judgment and righteousness in the earth. In His days Judah will be saved, and Israel will dwell safely; now this is His name by which He will be called: THE LORD OUR RIGHTEOUSNESS" (Jeremiah 23:5-6).

This prayer blessing for righteousness is as follows:

Restore our judges as in earliest times and our counselors as at first; remove from us sorrow and groan;

and reign over us—You, HASHEM, alone—with kindness and compassion, and justify us through judgment. Blessed are You, HASHEM, the King Who loves righteousness and judgment.

Blessing 12 – Destruction of God's Enemies

This blessing is difficult for Christians and needs to be clarified. It is like an interrupt or parenthesis in the sequence of prayers. It is basically a petition to the Almighty to destroy the enemies of the Jewish people. Some scholars believe it was written during the time of Ezra as a general judgment against any group considered to be heretical, such as the Samaritans, and even later the Sadducees.

The most accepted view, as stated earlier, is that Rabban Gamliel II had this composed around 90 AD as a curse on Jewish believers in Jesus. Until this time, the Jewish followers of Jesus continued to worship God in the synagogue. Obviously, they could not attend a synagogue service where they would have to pronounce a curse on themselves. Adding this nineteenth blessing to the *Amidah* forced Jewish believers in Jesus out of the synagogue and the traditional Jewish community.

With Jews living among the nations, it was necessary to change some of the original language. The word "heretics" was changed to say slanderers and wickedness and the phrase "uproot the evil government" was changed to say uproot wanton sinners. The blessing reads as follows:

And for slanderers let there be no hope; and may all wickedness perish in an instant; and may all Your enemies be cut down speedily. May You speedily uproot, smash, cast down, and humble the wanton sinners—speedily in our days. Blessed are You, HASHEM, Who break enemies and humbles wanton sinners.

Christians cannot accept a blessing that curses followers of Jesus. But we can ask the Almighty to destroy the enemies of Israel, which would be the proper application of the blessing today. This is the context of Psalm 83 which ends by saying, "Let them be confounded and dismayed forever; yes, let them be put to shame and perish, that they may know that You whose name alone is the LORD, are the Most High over all the earth" (Psalm 83:17-18). (See also Micah 4:11-12; Zephaniah 3:8; etc.)

Blessing 13 – Prayer for the Righteous

When justice prevails, the righteous are exalted. We wonder why God allows evil people to prosper and go unpunished. But the Bible assures us that God is just and there is a reward for the righteous. Moses explains, "He is the Rock, His work is perfect; for all His ways are justice, a God of truth and without injustice; righteous and upright is He" (Deuteronomy 32:4).

When God destroy the enemies of Israel, the people of God will say, "Surely there is a reward for the righteous; surely He is God who judges in the earth" (Psalm 58:11).

When God restores the fortunes of Israel and defeats her enemies, the righteous will be exalted and rewarded for their faithfulness to the God of Abraham, Isaac, and Jacob. The integrity of God's character and His word is our assurance that the righteous will prevail. This prayer blessing to the Almighty reads:

On the righteous, on the devout, on the elders of Your people the Family of Israel, on the remnant of their scholars, on the righteous converts and on ourselves—may Your compassion be aroused, HASHEM, our God, and give goodly reward to all who sincerely believe in Your Name. Put our lot with them forever, and we will not feel ashamed, for we trust in You. Blessed are You, HASHEM, Mainstay and Assurance of the righteous.

Blessing 14 – Rebuilding-Restoration of Jerusalem

For centuries the Jewish people have prayed, "Next year in Jerusalem." They have prayed and longed for the time when the Almighty would fulfill the words of the prophets who spoke of the day when God would restore Zion. Christian Zionists believe we are living in those days and that the liberation of Jerusalem in 1967 was a sign of it happening before our very eyes.

Psalm 147:2 reads, "The LORD builds up Jerusalem; He gathers together the outcasts of Israel. Psalm 102 reads, You will arise and have mercy on Zion; for the time to favor her, yes the set time has come. For the LORD shall build up Zion; He shall appear in His glory" (Psalm 102:13,16).

God gave the following word through the prophet Zechariah, "I am zealous for Zion with great zeal; with great fervor I am zealous for her. I will return to Zion, and dwell in the midst of Jerusalem …"(Zechariah 8:2-3).

This prayer blessing that we see being fulfilled in our generation reads as follows:

And to Jerusalem, Your city, may You return in compassion, and may You rest within it, as You have spoken. May You speedily establish the throne of David within it. Blessed are You, HASHEM, the Builder of Jerusalem.

Blessing 15 – Coming of Messiah-Davidic Reign

The final prayer blessing in this section on nationalistic promises is a prayer for the coming of Messiah at which time the kingdom of David will find its fullest expression. This represents the culmination of all the hopes of Jewish and Christian prayers for centuries. While we have different views regarding the Messiah, God will reconcile our differences when Messiah appears. Until then, Christians and Jews must work together for the security of Israel and the redemption of Jerusalem.

Amos writes, "On that day I will raise up the tabernacle of David, which has fallen down, and repair its damages; I will raise up its ruins, and rebuild it as in the days of old" (Amos 9:11).

This heart cry of the Jewish people for the Messiah is expressed as follows:

The offspring of Your servant David may You speedily cause to flourish, and enhance his pride through Your salvation, for we hope for Your salvation all day long. Blessed are You, HASHEM, Who causes the pride of salvation to flourish.

Blessing 16 – Summary Prayer of Acceptance

The worshipper concludes the petitions to God by calling on His compassion. God is gracious and full of mercy. The Hebrew words that best express these qualities are *hen* and *hesed*. They are translated into the English language by the familiar words "grace," "loving-kindness," and "mercy." The English word "grace" is found in the Hebrew Bible 38 times. Loving-kindness is mentioned 26 times and mercy is found 205 times.

Hear our voice, HASHEM our God, pity and be compassionate to us, and accept—with compassion and favor—our prayers, for God Who hears prayers and supplications are You. From before Yourself, our King, turn us not away empty handed, for You hear the prayer of Your people Israel with compassion. Blessed are You, HASHEM, Who hears prayer.

Blessing 17 – Restoration of Temple Worship

The last section of the *Amidah* contains three blessings. These are a plea for the rebuilding of the Temple and Temple worship, a prayer of thanksgiving, and a final prayer for peace.

Since the destruction of the Second Temple in 70 AD, Jews have longed for the building of the Third Temple at the coming of Messiah. While there are different theological views regarding the order of some of these end-time events, the prophets told of the time when the "House of the Lord" would be rebuilt on the Temple Mount and all nations would come to it and worship the God of Abraham, Isaac, and Jacob.

Isaiah writes, "Now it shall come to pass in the latter days that the mountain of the LORD'S house shall be established on the top of the mountains, and shall be exalted above the hills; and all nations shall flow to it. Many people shall come and say, 'Come, and let us go up to the mountain of the LORD, to the house of the God of Jacob; He will teach us His ways, and we will walk in His paths.' For out of Zion shall go forth the law, and the word of the LORD from Jerusalem" (Isaiah 2:2-3).

The Temple Institute in Jerusalem has made the garments for the High Priest and most of the vessels needed for Temple worship. We only await the perfect timing of the Almighty for this prayer blessing to be fulfilled.

Be favorable, HASHEM, our God, toward Your people Israel and their prayer and restore the service to the Holy of Holies of Your Temple. The fire-offerings of Israel and their prayer accept with love and favor, and may the service of Your people Israel always be favorable to You. Blessed are You, HASHEM, Who restores His presence to Zion.

Blessing 18 – Thanksgiving

After praising God and petitioning Him for our needs, we thank Him with a grateful heart for all that He is and all that He does for us. Psalm 92 reads, "It is good to give thanks to the LORD, and to sing praises to Your name, O Most High; to declare Your loving-kindness in the morning, and Your faithfulness every night" (Psalm 92:1-2). It is important to express gratitude to God and others who do things for us. We should not take for granted the One who is blessing nor the blessings He gives us.

We gratefully thank You, for it is You Who are HASHEM, our God and the God of our forefathers for all eternity; Rock of our lives, Shield of our salvation are You from generation to generation. We thank You from generation to generation. We shall thank You and relate Your praise—for our lives, which are committed to Your power and for our souls that are entrusted to You; for Your miracles that are with us every day; and for Your wonders and favors in every season—evening, morning, and afternoon. The Beneficent One, for Your compassions were never exhausted, and the Compassionate One, for Your kindness never ended—always have we put our hope in You.

For all these, may Your Name be blessed and exalted, our King, continually forever and ever. Everything alive will gratefully acknowledge You, Selah! And praise Your Name sincerely, O God of our salvation and help, Selah! Blessed are You, HASHEM, Your Name is 'the Beneficent One' and to You it is fitting to give thanks.

Blessing 19 – Peace

The last blessing in this great prayer is for God to manifest His presence and His peace to His people.

Establish peace, goodness, blessing, graciousness, kindness, and compassion upon us and upon all Your people Israel. Bless us, our Father, all of us as one, with the light of

Your countenance for with the light of Your countenance You gave us, HASHEM our God, the Torah of life and a love of kindness, righteousness, blessing, compassion, life, and peace. And may it be good in Your eyes to bless Your people Israel, in every season and in every hour with Your peace. Blessed are You, HASHEM, Who blesses His people Israel with peace.

Concluding Prayer

No matter how much we want to please God, we still need God's understanding and mercy to overlook our shortcomings when we pray. Therefore, the worshipper concludes his/her prayer for God to accept the prayer: "Let the words of my mouth and the mediation of my heart be acceptable in Your sight, O LORD, my strength and my Redeemer" (Psalm 19:14).

The Amidah for the Sabbath and Festivals

The *Amidah* for the Sabbath and Festivals is a much shorter prayer than the weekly *Amidah*. It consists of seven blessings. The first three and last three blessings are the same as the weekly prayer. The middle section is the shortened part of the prayer that emphasizes the sanctity of the day.

The oldest *Amidah* for the Sabbath in the times of Jesus was always the same. Later introductory paragraphs were added to the middle section.

Our God and the God of our fathers, may You be pleased with our rest. Sanctify us with Your commandments and grant our share in Your Torah; satisfy us from Your goodness and gladden us with Your salvation, and purify our heart to serve You sincerely. O HASHEM, our God, with love and favor grant us Your holy Sabbath as a heritage, and may Israel, the sanctifiers of Your Name, rest on it. Blessed are You, HASHEM, Who sanctifies the Sabbath.

3
The Jewish Background to the Lord's Prayer

In the two previous chapters, we learned that the Jewish people had prescribed prayers written by their leaders centuries before the time of Jesus. Two of the most ancient prayers were the *Shema* and the *Amidah*. Jews prayed these prayers at specified times at the Temple, the Synagogue and in the privacy of their homes. Jesus would have prayed these prayers, as well as His own personal prayers.

To keep prayer from becoming a meaningless ritual, teachers would help their students understand the true *kavanah* (spiritual intent) of prayer. Jesus' disciples were with Him when He prayed. They knew that John the Baptist taught his followers to pray. It was natural that they too ask Jesus to teach them to pray. We are grateful they asked Him because His answer has been preserved for our own learning.

Luke records the circumstances that led to the question. He writes, "Now it came to pass, as He was praying in a certain place, when He ceased, that one of His disciples said to Him, 'Lord, teach us to pray, as John also taught his disciples' "(Luke 11:1).

The "Lord's Prayer" is recorded in Matthew 6:9-13 and Luke 11:1-4. It is called the "Lord's Prayer" because Jesus taught it to His disciples. However, it is actually a prayer guide or model for the disciples. As stated previously, what Jesus taught His disciples was a summary of the true core *kavanah* of the *Amidah*. It is the heart and soul of true prayer that has come to us through the Jewish people.

Sometimes our prayers lack *kavanah.* Sometimes we pray without knowing what to say? Our prayers are often not answered. We may find ourselves praying as a ritual without really understanding the true meaning of what we are praying. As the disciples in the New Testament, we also need the Lord to teach us to pray. One of the most important lessons that will help us is understanding this most famous prayer in Christendom from its Hebraic context.

The Prayer

To keep the discussion simple, I will be referring to this model prayer as, "The Prayer." The Matthew version reads: "Our Father in heaven, Hallowed be Your name. Your kingdom come. Your will be done On earth as it is in heaven. Give us this day our daily bread. And forgive us our debts, as we forgive our debtors. And lead us not into temptation, But deliver us from the evil one. (For Yours is the kingdom and the power and the glory forever). Amen" (Matthew 6:9-13).

Our Father

The first part of "The Prayer" recognizes that God is personal. Unlike the pagan ideas of the gods, which were distant deities needing to be appeased; the God of the Bible is a Father. The Hebrews understood God to be a Father to them when He brought them out of Egypt.

One way Jewish fathers show their affection to their sons is by carrying them on their shoulders. I have seen this many times in Israel. God speaks in these "fatherly" terms to His people when He reminded them how He "carried them through the wilderness as a man carries his son" (Deuteronomy 1:31). Moses reminded the people of God's fatherly care with these words, "Is He not your Father, who bought you? Has He not made you and established you?" (Deuteronomy 32:6).

Because God is Father to the people as a covenant community, He is "Our Father." We learned in the first chapter that Jewish prayer is expressed within the context of community. Jewish people find their identification with their forefathers and the entire company of covenant people. This is why Jesus taught His disciples to pray as part of the whole people of God and not just for themselves.

Because human fathers are imperfect, many adults do not have a healthy relationship with their earthly father. However, our heavenly Father is perfect in His love, care, protection, provision, wisdom, and discipline. He is all we need in a father. If your relationship with your earthly father is lacking, cry out to your heavenly Father. He will fill that fatherly need in your life. King David understood this and wrote, "When my father and my mother forsake me, then the LORD will take care of me" (Psalm 27:10).

Jesus spoke of the fatherly care God has for His children. He said, "Or what man is there among you who, if his son asks for bread, will give him a stone? Or if he asks for a fish, will he give him a serpent? If you then, being evil, know how to give good gifts to your children, how much more will your Father who is in heaven give good things to those who ask Him" (Matthew 7:9-11)!

Christians are also part of a community of faith. God is not just our personal Father, He is the Father of all true believers. He is "Our Father." We are not only in covenant with God; we are in covenant with everyone else who is in covenant with God. We are brothers and sisters in the Lord. A New Testament phrase found 21 times is "one another." These one another expressions teach us the way people in covenant are to relate to each other. I encourage the reader to look these up as they give us the understanding of what Jesus meant when He said, "Our Father."

Our prayers, attitudes and actions should reflect this concept of community. In addition to praying for our personal needs, we should also have a sense that we are part of a family. Paul, the Jewish Apostle of our Lord, had this in mind when he wrote, "Let each one of you look out not only for his own interests, but also for the interest of others" (Philippians 2:4).

In Heaven

While the first part of "The Prayer" is intimate, the second phrase balances that intimacy with a reminder to us of Whom we are calling Father. He is our "Father in heaven." Our Father in heaven *(Avinu She-Ba-Shamayim)* was a common way the Jews addressed God based on Scriptures such as Isaiah 63:16; Jeremiah 31:9; Psalm 103:13; 1 Chronicles 29:10.

Now obviously Jesus knew were our Father God lives. So He was not thinking in terms of location. He was acknowledging the sovereign rule of God and His awesome holiness, greatness and majestic attributes of all-power, all-knowledge, everywhere presence, and unchanging nature.

Our Father in heaven, as opposed to our earthly fathers, is the self-existing, uncaused One who transcends time and space. He is the same yesterday, today, and tomorrow. He is limitless, measureless and boundless.

Our Father in heaven has no origin. He was not created, nor did He proceed from, or evolve out of, anything. In eternity past, God was alone. He was self-contained, self-sufficient, self-satisfied and in need of nothing. God was under no obligation to create anything. He chose to create as a sovereign act of His own will, determined by His own good pleasure and caused by nothing outside of Himself.

As the sovereign God, our Father in heaven is the supreme Lord and King of His universe. He actively exercises absolute rule over all His creation. He rules as the all-powerful One and every expression of power in the universe comes from Him.

Our Father in heaven not only rules absolutely with all-power, He also knows all things. God knows all that can be known, and he knows it instantly. He knows every possible item of knowledge concerning everything that could have existed, does exist or might exist anywhere in the universe, past, present and future. God knows all the possibilities, and He has chosen certain ones to take place out of the good pleasure of His sovereign will.

Our heavenly Father is everywhere present in His universe. He never has to go anywhere to find out what is going on because He's there already. He never has to be "somewhere" because He is everywhere, and at the same time. There never was a time when God wasn't everywhere. There never is a time when He isn't everywhere. And there never will be a time when He won't be everywhere. God has always been everywhere and always will be everywhere. We can never be lost from His presence.

Our Father in heaven is unchanging. He never has changed, is not now changing and never will change. He always was, always is and always will be the same in His person. What God was yesterday, He is today, and what He is today, He will be tomorrow.

Our Father in heaven is morally perfect in holiness, love, justice and goodness. He is altogether different from His creatures. His love is uncaused and transcends time and space. He is just and righteous is all His dealings with mankind. His goodness and mercy endures forever.

When we contemplate the greatness and goodness of God, we see why Jesus included the phrase, "in heaven." Our Father in heaven is different from our fathers on the earth. He is awesome in His majesty and perfect in His moral character. He is exactly the kind of Father we all need. Yet, His greatness and goodness requires and inspires a reverence and awe that acknowledges Him as Lord and King who is to be reverenced, worshipped and obeyed.

This opening teaching of "The Prayer" is very similar to an ancient Jewish prayer called the *Avinu Malkeinu*, which means, "Our Father, Our King." Jewish writings tell us that this prayer has its origins in the second century of our era and was spoken by Rabbi Akiva during a drought. The people prayed and fasted but there was no rain until Rabbi

Akiva poured out his heart to God with these words, "Our Father , our King, we have no king besides You. Our Father, our King, for Your own sake have mercy on us."

Jewish people still pray an extended version of this prayer during the high holy days from Rosh Hashanah to Yom Kippur and on different fast days. Each verse begins with the words, *Avinu Malkeinu* and is followed by an appeal to the Almighty to extend His mercy as a loving Father while acknowledging the responsibility of the worshipper to serve and obey God our King.

Hallowed Be Your Name

Once we grasp the spiritual reality that our Father is in heaven, that is, His awesome majesty and goodness, it follows that we would want to sanctify His name. This is the meaning behind the next phrase in "The Prayer."

Jesus taught the disciples to "hallow the name of God." What does this mean? The word "hallow" simply means to declare that God's name, which represents His character, is holy and should be sanctified in our lives. We sanctify God's name with our words and the way we live.

God is considered to be great and awesome because He is holy. This means He is set apart from His creation. Above all else, the Hebrews worshipped God for His holiness.

When God delivered them from Egypt, they sang the Song of Moses, "Who is like You, O LORD, among the gods? Who is like You, glorious in holiness, fearful in praises, doing wonders?" (Exodus 15:11).

God's works and ways are holy. His character is holy. His words and thoughts are holy. When someone in the Bible had an encounter with God, they were reduced to nothing. His holiness terrified them. His glory overwhelmed them. There was no pride, no ego, no arrogance and no self-exaltation left in one who had encountered the holy God. Our Father in heaven is holy.

No wonder the sages included a blessing to sanctify God's name as the third declaration in the *Amidah.* To review, it reads, *You are holy and Your name is holy, and holy ones praise You every day, forever. Blessed are You, HASHEM, the holy God.*

Only God is naturally holy. But whatever or whoever He has set apart to Himself is also holy by the very act of God setting something or someone apart. God said to His people, "And you shall be to Me a kingdom of priests and a holy nation" (Exodus 19:6). He emphasized this to His people, "You shall be holy, for I the LORD your God am holy" (Leviticus 19:2).

God's holiness is seen in His people. To hallow God's name does not just mean to say some words in a creed or in a prayer. It means to live a holy life. God has chosen us to be a holy people. We are a people set apart and different from those around us who do not know the Holy One of Israel.

We are to be in the world but not of this world. We are God's people. We are a separate people. We have received the Holy Spirit who transforms us into the image of our holy God. We yield our spirit to His Spirit. We renew our minds with His thoughts and set our will and emotions towards Him. We give our bodies as holy vessels containing the glory of God.

We are to let His holy light shine through us and live as the salt of the earth (Matthew 5:13-16). When we live in this way, God's holiness is seen in us. His name is sanctified in His people.

Your Kingdom Come, Your Will Be Done

Because our Father in heaven is holy, we pray, live and work to sanctify His name and bring His kingdom and His will to pass. This part of "The Prayer" also comes from ancient Jewish prayers that Jesus would have prayed.

The concept of the Kingdom of God or the Kingdom of Heaven (both phrases mean the same) is central to the Jewish views of God, and their relationship to Him. God is not just the Redeemer-Savior, He is the Sovereign King who rules over His creation. That includes His people.

When God delivered the Hebrews out of Egypt, they declared, "The LORD shall reign forever and ever" (Exodus 15:18). The writer of Psalms exhorts the people to praise God with these words, "Sing praise to God, sing praises! Sing praises to our King, sing praises! For God is the King of all the earth; sing praises with understanding. God reigns over the nations; God sits on His holy throne" (Psalm 47:6-8).

When the sages composed their prayers to God, they included His Kingship as a central part of their blessing. As we learned earlier, each blessing begins with the declaration, *Blessed are You O LORD our God, King of the universe.*

The prayer declaration, *Blessed is the name of His glorious kingdom forever and ever* is basically the same affirmation of Jesus' words, "Your Kingdom Come."

Those that God called to Himself became part of His kingdom and were to live under His rule. God explained, "And you shall be to Me a kingdom of priests and a holy nation … "(Exodus 19:6).

Jesus' meaning of the Kingdom of God-Heaven is one of the most misunderstood of His teachings. To the Jewish mind, the Kingdom of God was not some event that would happen in the distant future. It was a present reality that would culminate at the end of the age. When Jesus spoke of the Kingdom of God being "at hand" (Matthew 4:17), He meant it was now being realized through the demonstration and manifestation of the power and rule of God as seen in His miracles.

Matthew writes, "And Jesus went about all Galilee, teaching in their synagogues, preaching the gospel of the Kingdom, and healing all kinds of sickness and all kinds of disease among the people" (Matthew 4:23). Jesus told His followers to, "seek first the kingdom of God …"(Matthew 6:33). He sent them to preach the gospel of the kingdom (Matthew 10:7).

We see this same idea in the first praise in the Kaddish, *May His great Name grow exalted and sanctified in the world that He created as He willed. May He give reign to His kingship in your lifetimes and in your days, and in the lifetimes of the entire family of Israel, swiftly and soon. Amen.* May He give reign to His kingship expresses the same thought as, "Your kingdom come."

A feature of Hebrew poetry is parallelism. Hebrew parallelism couples several phrases so that the second phrase amplifies, reinforces and clarifies the first phrase. In the case of "The Prayer," the phrase, "May Your will be done," is like an exclamation point emphasizing and clarifying the meaning of, "Your kingdom come." God's kingdom is realized when God's people do His will.

Jesus made the same point when He said, "Not everyone who says to Me, 'Lord, Lord' shall enter the kingdom of heaven, but he who does the will of My Father in heaven" (Matthew 7:21).

God has a will and purpose for creation in general and our lives in particular. He desires to bring His will from heaven to earth. We can know God's will because He has written it for us in the Bible. God wants us to know His will and pray it from heaven to earth. Then, under His Kingship, we give ourselves in partnership with God to do His will.

Rabbi Feuer writes, "Prayer is not a duel, a struggle between two opposing wills, rather it is an attempt to achieve a merger of wills. Indeed, our prayers are an opportunity to yield ourselves to His will, but by virtue of our submission to God, we can hope that He will grant our plea. As our Sages taught: 'Treat His will as if it were your will, so that He will treat your will as if it were His will. Nullify your will before His will, so that He will nullify the will of others before your will' (Avos 2:4) (Shemoneah Esrei, page 16).

Rabbi Feuer includes the following comment on partnering with God, "Reb Yerucham states that the reason the great *tzaddikim* were able to make things happen with their prayers was because they had achieved a status of being "partners with God" in the operation of the world. As partners, they had an authoritative position.

"If we think our prayers are not effective enough, perhaps we should think of conducting our lives in such a way that God accords us the status of "partnership." This is not an easy achievement, but we are then in a position not only to pray, but actually demand of God that He reveal His glory in the world, and openly sanctify His name so that all living things can see His majesty" (page 87).

The Western Christian understanding of "Your kingdom come" relates to time. We think of it in terms of the coming of Jesus at the end of the age. While all true believers are waiting for this blessed event (even so, come Lord Jesus), Jesus had something entirely different in mind. He desires to manifest His kingdom in our present world

Jesus did not preach our Western, easy-to-believe, gospel of salvation. He preached a very Jewish message of the gospel of the Kingdom. Failure to understand this is one of the major reasons why Western Christianity has lacked the power of God and been so ineffective. Our moral light is dim. Our spiritual salt has lost its savior. Where there is no root, there is no fruit. This is just one of many unfortunate results of the loss of our Hebraic roots.

But we can be encouraged that God is awakening us to this reality. As we rediscover our roots, we will bear much fruit. Our light will once again shine bright. Our salt with regain its savor. The glory of God will cover the earth as the waters cover the sea. Jesus explained it this way, "And this gospel of the kingdom will be preached in all the world as a witness to all the nations, and then the end will come" (Matthew 41:14).

Jesus meant for us to understand that our Father in heaven is not just our Redeemer-Savior. He is our Sovereign Lord and King who desires to demonstrate and manifest His rule in our lives. When we acknowledge Him as Lord, we take on the yoke of His kingdom. By doing His will, we are partnering with Him to bring His kingdom/will from heaven to earth as a present reality. His name is sanctified and His kingdom is realized through His people living under His rule.

Give Us This Day Our Daily Bread

Once we worship God and invite His rule in our life, we have the right to ask and expect Him to meet our personal needs. *Avinu Malkeinu* is a faithful, covenant-keeping God.

When we accept the yoke of His kingdom, we become stewards of our life. We are no longer living for ourselves. We are living to bring forth the part of the kingdom of God that He has entrusted into our hands. We are not owners; we are stewards. We are accountable to God to administer the resources He gives us with excellence and integrity. But God is responsible to give us what we need. So Jesus instructed us to pray, *Give us this day our daily bread.*

A Scripture in Proverbs helps us better understand what Jesus meant. It says, "... Give me neither poverty nor riches—feed me with the food allotted to me" (Proverbs 30:8). The Hebrew word for food in this verse is *lechem*. It is the word for bread, which can be used in its broadest sense, to refer to our needs in general. Jesus was teaching us that God has allotted or allocated to us a portion of His resources we need to fulfill His kingdom will for our lives. He is faithful to give us what we need.

In Matthew 6:25-34, Jesus told His disciples not to worry about material things. He said, "For after all these things the Gentiles seek. For your heavenly Father knows that you need all these things. But seek first the kingdom of God and His righteousness, and all these things shall be added to you" (Matthew 6:32-33).

And Forgive Us Our Debts as We Forgive Our Debtors

Whereas the gods of the pagans were unmerciful, the God of the Bible is a God of mercy who understands the failures of His children and is eager to forgive them when they sin. Because of his own sins, King David often praised God for His mercy. He wrote, "Bless the LORD, O my soul, and forget not all His benefits: who forgives all your iniquities, who heals all your diseases, who redeems your life from destruction, Who crowns you with loving-kindness and tender mercies" (Psalm 103:3-4).

The Hebrew Scriptures are filled with thanksgiving to God for His mercy and forgiveness. *Hesed* is most often translated by the English word mercy and is found 205 times in the Hebrew Bible. The psalmists writes, "Oh, give thanks to the LORD, for He is good! For His mercy endures forever" (Psalm 106:1)

It is no wonder that when the men of the Great Synagogue composed the *Amidah,* they included the sixth blessing which says, *Forgive us, our Father, for we have erred; pardon us, our King, for we have willfully sinned; for You pardon and forgive. Blessed are You, HASHEM, the gracious One Who forgives abundantly.*

Jesus certainly understood our weaknesses and the need we have for forgiveness. He addressed this need and included it as part of His core summary of ancient Jewish prayers. He taught us to pray, "And forgive us our debts, as we forgive our debtors." In Luke's version of "The Prayer," we learn that the word translated as debt should be sins or trespasses.

Biblical Judaism emphasized that until a person is right in their relationships with others, they cannot be right in their relationship with their heavenly Father. Jesus did not give a new "Christian" thought in this element of "The Prayer" but simply confirmed the basic Jewish understanding that one cannot be right with God if they are not right with their fellow man.

Our heavenly Father is quick to forgive us our sins but only if we forgive others who have sinned against us. Jesus explains, "For if you forgive men their trespasses, your heavenly Father will also forgive you. But if you do not forgive men their trespasses, neither will your Father forgive your trespasses" (Matthew 6:14-15).

Jesus told a powerful story to illustrate this in the parable of the Unforgiving Servant (Matthew 18:23-35). In the parable, a servant owed his master a large sum of money. When the master demanded payment, the servant begged for mercy because he was not able to pay the debt. The master was moved with compassion and forgave him the debt. Then the servant went and demanded payment from those who owed him money. When they couldn't pay, they too asked for mercy. But the servant threw them in jail. When the master heard how the servant showed no mercy, he then demanded payment from the unforgiving servant.

Jesus ends the story be saying, "So My heavenly Father also will do to you if each of you, from his heart, does not forgive his brother his trespasses" (Matthew 18:5).

One of the sacrificial offerings given in the Bible is the trespass offering. When a person sinned, they were to bring a ram and offer it as a trespass offering. If their sin harmed someone, they were to make restitution. If they brought the sacrifice to God but did make restitution with the offended party, God did not accept their sacrifice.

Jesus referred to this and said, "Therefore if you bring your gift to the altar, and there remember that your brother has something against you, leave your gift there before the altar, and go your way. First be reconciled to your brother, and then come and offer your gift"(Matthew 5:23-24).

Jesus gave us the ultimate human example of the power and need for forgiveness. His last prayer from the cross was, "Father forgive them, for they do not know what they do …"(Luke 23:34).

Our heavenly Father is the only One who has never done anything wrong. Yet, He has chosen to show mercy and forgive. How much more should we, who have done much wrong, forgive those who have offended us. Since God has forgiven us a great debt of sin, we certainly should forgive others the relatively small debt of sin they owe us.

And Lead Us Not Into Temptation But Deliver Us From The Evil One

Our heavenly Father has called us into His kingdom. He has revealed His will for our lives and entrusted a portion of His kingdom resources into our hands. Therefore, Jesus instructs us to pray that we would not be led into temptation and overcome by evil. This is also a Hebrew parallelism in which the second line clarifies and reinforces the first line.

While we are all tempted, the thought Jesus is presenting is that we will not be overcome by the temptation. We are praying that God will deliver us from the power of sin and Satan. This plea for divine assistance is also a part of ancient Jewish prayers. The Psalmist pleaded to God, "Direct my steps by Your Word, and let no iniquity have dominion over me. Redeem me from the oppression of man, that I may keep Your precepts. Make Your face shine upon Your servant, and teach me your statutes" (Psalm 119:133-135).

We learn from this Scripture that the way we overcome evil is by meditating on the Word of God. The Holy Spirit uses God's Word to cleanse us of sin and empower us to live a kingdom lifestyle. The Psalmist wrote, "How can a young man cleanse his way? By taking heed according to Your word. With my whole heart I have sought You; O let me not wander from Your commandments! Your word I have hidden in my heart, that I might not sin against You" (Psalm 119:9-11).

Judaism teaches that we all have a good inclination *(yetzer tov)* and a bad inclination *(yetzer hara)*. The Christian understanding is that the good inclination is the power of the

Holy Spirit working in us while the bad inclination is our sinful nature. Jesus is simply instructing us to allow the Holy Spirit to rule in our lives so that we will not be overcome by sin and satanic influences.

The Jewish apostle Paul expressed the same thought with these words, "No temptation has overtaken you except such as is common to man; but God is faithful, who will not allow you to be tempted beyond what you are able, but with the temptation will also make the way of escape, that you may be able to bear it" (1 Corinthians 10:13).

Our heavenly Father is just the kind of father we need. He is awesome and fearful in His majesty and glory but gracious and merciful in dealing with His children. He calls us to acknowledge Him as King and Lord and sanctify His name through our words and deeds. We take on the yoke of His kingdom and are His stewards on the earth. We are accountable to do His will with integrity and excellence.

He is responsible to meet our needs. We forgive those who have offended us as He has forgiven us. We meditate on His word and ask the Holy Spirit to empower us so we can fulfill His kingdom purposes for our lives.

The Jewish Lord's Prayer

"The Prayer" is a very Jewish prayer. It has come to us from the lips of our Jewish Lord. May we be better children of our heavenly Father as we learn to pray the prayers of Jesus.

The closing words of praise, "For Yours is the kingdom and the power and the glory forever," do not appear in some of the ancient manuscripts of the New Testament. Yet, they are similar to King David's final words of praise to God as recorded in 1 Chronicles. Therefore, it is proper to close this writing with this praise to our heavenly Father.

"Blessed are You, LORD God of Israel, our father, forever and ever. Yours O LORD is the greatness, the power and the glory, the victory and the majesty; for all that is in heaven and in earth is Yours; Yours is the kingdom, O LORD, and You are exalted as head above all. Both riches and honor come from You, and You reign over all. In Your hand is power and might; in Your hand it is to make great and to give strength to all. Now therefore, our God, we thank You and praise Your glorious name" (1 Chronicles 29:10-13).

Praying in the Name of Jesus

Christians end their prayers by saying, "in Jesus' name." This can be a concern when praying with Jewish friends. We want to be sensitive and not offend, but at the same time we must be true to what we believe. Learning the Hebraic roots of Christianity can help us with this concern.

In Bible times, a person's name represented the character of the person. To do something in someone's name was to do it in their character with their purposes and intent in mind. To pray in Jesus' name relates to our lives, not our lips. We would be more biblical for Christians to end our prayers by saying something like, "Father may Your name and will be sanctified through this prayer and in my life." .

About the Author

Dr. Richard Booker is a Bible teacher and author known for his ability to communicate difficult subjects in an easy-to-understand manner. He has written many best-selling books which have touched the lives of people around the world.

In 1974, God dramatically changed Richard's life while he was studying the book of Leviticus. He saw Jesus in every book of the Bible. Afterwards, Richard left his successful business career to teach and write about the insights God was giving him.

Richard, along with his wife, Peggy, travel extensively sharing God's Word with clarity and love to both Christians and Jews. *If you would like for Richard to come to your church, congregation, conference or study group, contact him at his Houston address.*

Dr. Booker has written 38 books and developed 19 college level courses on the Bible from a Judeo-Christian perspective. He has also made over 500 Christian television programs and serves as a spiritual father to many, He and Peggy have led tour groups to Israel for 25 years, where for 18 years, Dr. Booker was a featured teacher for the international Christian celebration of the Feast of Tabernacles in Jerusalem

Richard is the founder of Sounds of the Trumpet, Inc. and the Institute for Hebraic-Christian Studies (IHCS). IHCS provides courses on the Hebraic roots of Christian leading to a Diploma in Hebraic-Christian Studies. *Contact him to learn more about you can take these life-changing courses.*

Richard has an M.B.A. and a Ph. D. in Theology.

Books on the Hebraic-Jewish Roots of Christianity

by Dr. Booker

Here Comes the Bride

One of the most beautiful pictures of God's love is the ancient Jewish wedding. This book explains Jewish wedding customs and how they point to the Messiah as well as what we can do to prepare ourselves for the greatest event of the ages, the wedding of God's bride.

Shabbat Shalom

While the Sabbath is central in Jewish life, many Christians are being called by God to discover the Jewish roots of their faith. This publication explains what the Bible says about the Sabbath and how Christians can celebrate the Sabbath in their own homes.

How the Cross Became a Sword

This book explains the events that separated Christianity from its Jewish roots and established anti-Semitism as official church doctrine. It then gives an excellent overview of the tragic history of Christian-Jewish relations directly linking modern replacement theology to the first Christian

Islam, Christianity, and Israel

This book reveals the shocking information about the life of Mohammed and the background, teachings and practices of Islam. The reader learns how Islam differs from Christianity and the truth about the conflict between the Arabs and the Jews which you won't learn from the news.

The Time to Favor Zion Has Come

One of the greatest events of our times is the rebirth of the State of Israel. This book explains the prophetic aspects of the final ingathering of the Jewish people back to their land in preparation for the coming of Messiah. You will learn how the Jews are being regathered, restored, and redeemed.

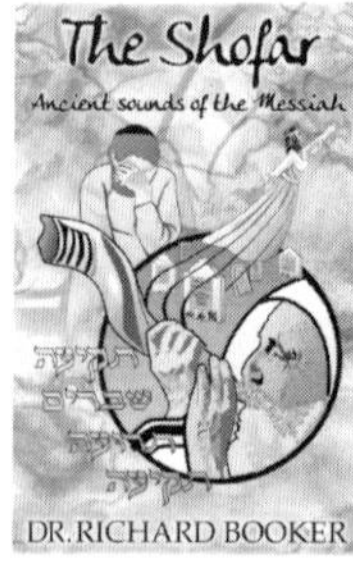

The Shofar: Ancient Sounds of the Messiah

This book explains the background, purposes, and use of the shofar in ancient and modern times and how the shofar called the people to a deeper walk with God through the Messiah.

Blow the Trumpet in Zion

This book explains the dramatic and fascinating story of the Jewish people, Israel and the nation in prophecy. It is one of the most comprehensive books relating Bible prophecy to world history and current and future events as they revolve around God's covenant plan for Israel.

Celebrating Jesus in the Biblical Feasts

This is a study of the Feasts of the Lord showing how they pointed to Jesus and their personal and prophetic significance for today's world. It reveals how the Feasts represents seven steps in the believer's walk with God.

The Miracle of the Scarlet Thread

This is a worldwide best-selling classic on the blood covenant and how it pictures the Messiah in connecting the two Testaments in the Bible to tell one complete story. It is considered standard reading for believers around the world.

No Longer Strangers

This is a comprehensive introduction to the Hebraic-Jewish roots of Christianity. The text is well-documented with footnotes, a helpful bibliography, and an index for easy reference. Dr. Booker explains Christian and Jewish history, beliefs and practices, how Christianity and Judaism relate, and more.

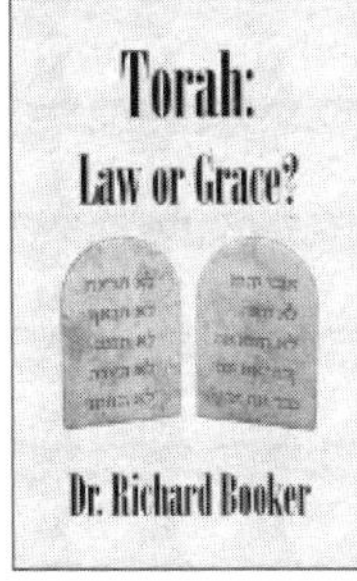

Torah: Law or Grace

This is one of the most eye-opening books you will ever read. You will discover the true meaning of law and grace, how these powerful words have been misunderstood, the prophetic restoration of their true meaning, and the significance this has for

ORDER at www.rbooker.com or call 936-441-2171

Ancient Jewish Prayers and the Messiah

This profound book will revolutionize your life. You will discover the Jewish background to Christian prayers, the Jewish background to the "Lord's Prayer" and the most important prayer in Judaism that concerns events regarding the restoration of Jerusalem and the coming of Messiah.

Discovering The Miracle of the Scarlet Thread in Every Book of the Bible

This book takes the mystery out of the Bible as Dr. Booker explains the master theme of the Bible showing Jesus and the blood covenant story in every book of the Bible.

The Root and Branches

This is an orientation course for those just beginning their study of the Jewish roots of Christianity. It is Jewish Roots 101.

For more information on these and other life-changing books by Dr. Booker, see his web site and online store at www.rbooker.com

UNDERSTANDING THE BOOK OF REVELATION

In this groundbreaking three-volume series, Dr. Booker helps you understand the Book of Revelation by explaining John's vision within its intriguing original historical, literary, and biblical context. In this inspiring and informative series, you will understand John's Revelation and its meaning for you today.

THE OVERCOMERS

(BOOK 1 OF 3) ***Revelation Chapters 1-3***

The Book of Revelation is not a book of doom and gloom but the *victory* of the Lamb of God and those who follow Him *The Overcomers*.

THE LAMB AND THE SEVEN-SEALED SCROLL

(BOOK 2 OF 3) ***Revelation Chapters 4-12***

Dr. Booker turns his clear, prophetic explanation to the seven-sealed scroll, which contains the word of the Lord given to Daniel and is sealed until the time of the end.

THE VICTORIOUS KINGDOM

(BOOK 3 OF 3) ***Revelation Chapters 13-22***

In this third book in a groundbreaking series, Dr. Richard Booker explains John's vision within its original historical, literary, and biblical context.

The End of All Things Is at Hand Are You Ready?

Dr. Booker avoids the sensational and writes to touch your heart. He explains biblical prophecy and current and future events from a biblical Hebraic world view rather than a traditional, Western cultural world view.

ORDER at www.rbooker.com or call 936-441-2171